INDEPENDENT STUDY PROGRAM

Student Booklet

Susan K. Johnsen
Baylor University

Kay Johnson
Educational Consultant

ISBN 1-882664-17-5

PRUFROCK PRESS

P.O. Box 8813 ▼ Waco ▼ TX ▼ 76714 ▼ (817) 756-3337 ▼ FAX (817) 756-3339

TABLE OF CONTENTS

I'M JUST MOVING CLOUDS TODAY ••

• TOMORROW I'LL TRY MOUNTAINS •

Ashleigh Brilliant

WHAT IS INDEPENDENT STUDY?

> Independent study is the process
> which you apply when you research
> a new topic by yourself or with others.

Check each step that you use in your independent study. You will find more help with each step by using the Resource Cards.

INDEPENDENT STUDY STEP	RESOURCE CARDS
___1. Select a Topic	2 - 4
___2. Organize a Topic	5 - 9
___3. Ask Questions	10 - 14
___4. Use a Study Method	15 - 32
___5. Collect Information	33 - 62
___6. Develop a Product	63 - 91
___7. Present Information	92 - 96
___8. Evaluate the Study	97

INDEPENDENT STUDY PLAN

NAME _____ DATE STARTED _____

TEACHER _____ DATE DUE _____

GENERAL INFORMATION   DATE DUE

   1. Name of Topic_____   _____

   2. Organization_____   _____

   3. Specific Question_____   _____

           _____

   4. Method of Study_____   _____

COLLECT INFORMATION

___ Books	___ Field Trips	___ Filmstrips
___ Interviews	___ Collections	___ Reference Books
___ Surveys	___ Letters	___ Observations
___ Experiments	___ Magazines	___ Museums
___ Movies/Films	___ Newspapers	___ T.V./Radio

   ___ Other:_____

The end of reading is not more books but more life ··· H. Jackson

DEVELOP THE PRODUCT   DATE DUE

1. Audience

__ My Class   __ Competition

__ My School   __ Other: _____

2. Product Plan

__ Journal	__ Booklet	__ T.V. Show
__ Model	__ Display	__ Written Report
__ Slide Show	__ Collection	__ Shadow Box
__ Poster	__ Game	__ Puppet Show
__ Graph	__ Diagram	__ Tape Recording
__ Chart	__ Play	__ Time Line

__ Other: _____

3. Final Product   _____

PRESENT THE PRODUCT   _____

EVALUATE THE STUDY

__ Self   __ Teacher

__ Others _____   _____

WHAT IS A TOPIC?

A topic is the name of the subject or the main idea that you will study. Topics help you organize and classify large pieces of information into a word or phrase.

How do I choose a topic?

- A problem I want to solve is _____

  _____

- A fact I want to prove is _____

  _____

- Something I want to learn to do is _____

  _____

- Something I want to know more about is _____

  _____

- Other topics that interest me are _____

  _____

HOW DO I EVALUATE THE TOPICS?

1.   Select five topics to judge. Write these topics on the lines.

2.   Think of some reasons (criteria) by which you will judge your topics.

3.   Decide on three criteria and write them on the lines at the top of the chart by "A," "B," and "C."

4.   Look at the first reason (Criterion A). Ask the question and then put a "5" in the box next to the topic that best fits the criterion. Put a "4" next to the topic that is next best. Do the same with the numbers "3," "2," and "1." Next, look at the second question (Criterion B). Follow the same process for Criterion B and Criterion C.

5.   Add the numbers next to each topic and put the sum in the *Total* box. The highest total may be the best topic to study. Write it on your Independent Study Plan (ISP).

EXAMPLE:

C.   Which is the most interesting topic?

CRITERIA   **B.**   Which is the most useful topic?

A.   Which will have information easy to find?

T O T A L

TOPICS	A	B	C	
1. advertising				
2. photography				
3. oceanography				
4. pollution				
5. robotics				

adapted from Texas Future Problem Solving

TOPIC EVALUATION CHART

Directions: Follow the example on SB 5. Write the reasons you might study a topic beside **A, B,** and **C.** List five topics on the lines. Read Criterion A and put a "5" beside the topic that best fits that reason. Put a "4" by the next best topic, and so on to "1." Rank topics using Criteria B and C in the same way.

CRITERIA

C. _____

B. _____

A. _____

T O T A L

TOPICS	A	B	C	
1._____				
2._____				
3._____				
4._____				
5._____				

adapted from Texas Future Problem Solving

WHAT IS TOPIC ORGANIZATION?

> **Organizing a topic means to arrange
> it in a way which will help you
> find specific questions to ask.**

How do I organize a topic?

You will organize your topic in one or more of the following ways:

_____1. **Describe** your topic in one or more ways.

_____2. **Compare** your topic to something else.

_____3. Identify possible **causes and effects** which have influenced the topic.

_____4. Describe **problems and solutions** which relate to the topic.

Before you check the way you want to organize your topic, you will want to look at Resource Cards 5 - 9. These cards show an example of each way to organize a topic.

LET'S ORGANIZE THIS THING···
·AND TAKE ALL THE FUN OUT OF IT·

Ashleigh
Brilliant

WHAT IS A GOOD STUDY QUESTION?

A good study question...

1. Requires more than one answer
2. Might have different answers from different people
3. Needs time to be studied
4. Has information available for study
5. Is useful or beneficial

EXAMPLES:

Poor Study Question:
How many students are in my school?

Good Study Question:
How do students in my school feel about intermural sports?

Which are good study questions?

Directions: Write a "P" or a "G" in front of each question to tell if it is a poor or good study question.

_____ 1. What is the story of *Huckleberry Finn* ?

_____ 2. Do students who get "A's" in school study more than students who get "B's?"

_____ 3. Which living creatures are in danger of becoming extinct?

_____ 4. How many different kinds of whales are there?

_____ 5. How do children learn to talk?

_____ 6. What were the most important changes in your school in the last five years?

_____ 7. Why do animals migrate?

_____ 8. How is pollution controlled in different parts of the world?

_____ 9. What kinds of equipment are used at a weather station?

_____ 10. What does my teacher think about recycling paper products?

LITTLE THINKING QUESTIONS

WHO

WHAT

WHERE

WHEN

WHY

HOW

MORE THINKING QUESTIONS

WHO

WHAT

WHERE

WHEN

WHY

HOW

MOST THINKING QUESTIONS

WHO

WHAT

WHERE

WHEN

WHY

HOW

HOW DO I EVALUATE A STUDY QUESTION?

1. Select five questions to judge. Write these questions on the lines by the numbers.

2. Think of some reasons (criteria) by which you will judge your questions. For example, is the question of use or benefit to someone? Is the question interesting to me? Will I be able to find information about it?

3. Decide on three criteria and write them on the lines at the top of the chart by "A," "B," and "C."

4. Look at the first reason (criterion A). Put a "5" in the box next to the question that best fits criterion A. Put a "4" next to the question that is next best. Do the same with the numbers "3," "2," and "1." Follow the same process with the second reason (criterion B) and the third reason (criterion C).

5. Add the numbers next to each question and put the sum in the **Total** box. The highest total may be your best question to study.

EXAMPLE:

QUESTION EVALUATION CHART

C. The question requires the most thinking.

CRITERIA   **B.** The question will be most beneficial to others in the future.

                A. The question is the most interesting to me.

QUESTIONS	A	B	C	T O T A L
1. How might I develop a way to protect endangered wildlife?				
2. How are birds' and mammals' habits alike and different?				
3. In what ways are plant and animal development the same or different?				
4. Do animals and humans develop communication systems in the same way?				
5. What might be a good way to evaluate zoos?				

adapted from Texas Future Problem Solving

QUESTION EVALUATION CHART

Directions: Follow the example on SB 12. Write the reasons you might develop a study question beside Criteria A, B, and C. List five study questions on the lines below. Read criterion A and put a "5" beside the question that best matches that reason. Put a "4" by the next best question, and so on to "1." Rank questions using Criteria B and C in the same way.

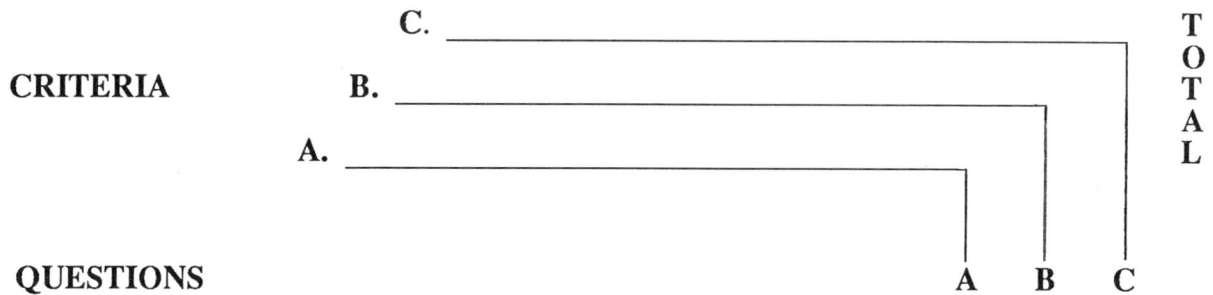

CRITERIA	C. _____			TOTAL
	B. _____			
	A. _____			

QUESTIONS	A	B	C	
1.				
2.				
3.				
4.				
5.				

adapted from Texas Future Problem Solving

I HAVE A THEORY THAT IT'S IMPOSSIBLE TO PROVE ANYTHING:

BUT I CAN'T PROVE IT

WHAT IS A STUDY METHOD?

A study method describes
certain steps that you will follow
when you study your questions.

Identify one of these methods you will use in your study:

_____1. I will describe something with numbers or facts.

_____2. I will look at the past or history of my topic.

_____3. I will look at changes or the development of my topic.

_____4. I will observe a person, group or thing closely.

_____5. I will compare one thing with another thing using numbers.

_____6. I will examine an improvement I made to solve a problem.

_____7. I will set up an experiment and look at the results.

_____8. I will collect factual information.

Before you check the way you want to study your questions, you will want to look at Resource Cards 15 - 32. These cards show an example of each way.

*The formulation
of a problem
is often
more important
than its
solution*
—Einstein

WHERE DO I COLLECT INFORMATION?

Information can be gathered in a variety of ways: brainstorming, classifying, interviewing, taking notes of material read or heard, summarizing and surveying. You can probably think of many more. In the space below, list all the **specific** places you could go and people you could contact to collect some information about your topic.

WHAT IS A PRODUCT?

> **A product is something that you will do or make
> to give information to others about the subject
> you have researched.**

Brainstorm products!

List all the possible products you can imagine that might convey information about your study. Don't think alone! Ask others; work with a team; keep the ideas flowing.

·IMAGINATION··
·NOT INVENTION·
·IS THE SUPREME·
·MASTER OF ART·
·AS A LIFE·
·CONRAD·

HOW DO I SELECT THE BEST PRODUCT?

1. On the lines beside "A," "B," and "C", list some possible products you are considering (see example).

2. By the numbers, list some reasons why you might develop a product.

3. Look at the first reason (Criterion A) and put a "5" in the box next to the product that best fits the reason. Put a "4" for the product that fits next best, and so on to "1" for the product that fits least best. Follow the same process with the second reason (Criterion B) and the third reason (Criterion C).

4. Add the numbers next to each product and enter the sum in the *Total* column. The product with the *largest* total may be the best product to develop.

EXAMPLE:

PRODUCT EVALUATION CHART

C. Which will give the audience the most information?

QUESTIONS   B. Which will be the most interesting for me?   T O T A L

A. Which will be the most unusual?

PRODUCTS	A	B	C	TOTAL
1. book (illustrated)				
2 written report with graph				
3. oral report with display				
4. board game				
5. chart of survey results				

adapted from Texas Future Problem Solving

PRODUCT EVALUATION CHART

Directions: Complete the following chart to help you select the best product. Follow the example on SB 17. Write the reasons you might choose a product beside Criteria A, B, and C. List five products on the lines below. Read Criterion A and put a "5" beside the product that best matches that reason. Put a "4" beside the next best product, and so on to "1." Rank products using Criteria B and C in the same way. Remember, the *highest* score should be the best product for you to develop.

C. _____

QUESTIONS   B. _____   T
O
A. _____   T
A
L

PRODUCTS   A   B   C

PRODUCTS	A	B	C	TOTAL
1.				
2.				
3.				
4.				
5.				

adapted from Texas Future Problem Solving

WHAT IS A PRODUCT PLAN?

> **A product plan is a system used in planning and developing the product.**

The plan should include...

1. a list of steps to follow to complete the product.
2. all materials needed to develop the product.
3. an approximate amount of time needed for each step.

In the space below, draw a sketch of how you want your final product to look.

PRODUCT PLAN

Complete the chart below, filling in steps you need to follow in order to develop the product.

STEPS **TIME NEEDED**

_____

_____

_____

_____

_____

_____

_____

_____

MATERIALS NEEDED

_____

_____

_____

_____

PLEASE··
DON·T SUPPLY
ANY MORE
INFORMATION·
·

I·M ALREADY
TOO WELL
INFORMED·:

Ashleigh
Brilliant

HOW DO I PRESENT THE PRODUCT?

PRESENTATION CHECKLIST

		YES	NO
1.	Have I prepared the materials (handouts, overhead transparencies, display, *etc.*) needed in my presentation?	____	____
2.	Have I practiced my presentation out loud (in front of a mirror or in front of another person)?	____	____
3.	Have I timed my talk?	____	____
4.	Have I made brief notes on index cards of the main ideas I will discuss?	____	____
5.	When I practiced my presentation, did I...		
a.	speak loudly enough for the audience to hear?	____	____
b.	tell the topic and study question?	____	____
c.	glance at my notes **only** when I needed them?	____	____
d.	show the display or materials smoothly along with my talk?	____	____
e.	ask if there are any questions?	____	____
f.	thank the audience for listening?	____	____

The final performance
which may take a minute
has been preceded by
many hours of rehearsal
L.P. Smith

SELF EVALUATION

Name _____ Date _____

Topic _____

Directions: Circle the number that best reflects your feelings about each statement.

	DISAGREE				AGREE
I had a well planned independent study.	1	2	3	4	5
I used my time efficiently.	1	2	3	4	5
I wrote a probing study question.	1	2	3	4	5
I used varied resources.	1	2	3	4	5
My research was extensive.	1	2	3	4	5
I developed a fine product.	1	2	3	4	5
My class presentation was effective.	1	2	3	4	5
I have good feelings about the independent study.	1	2	3	4	5

What I did well: _____

_____

The most difficult part was: _____

_____

What I would change: _____

_____

take a second look...

it costs you nothing.

Chinese proverb

TEACHER'S EVALUATION

Name _____ Date _____

Topic _____

Directions: Circle the number that best reflects your feelings about each statement.

	DISAGREE				AGREE
Student had a well planned independent study.	1	2	3	4	5
Student used time efficiently.	1	2	3	4	5
Student wrote a probing study question.	1	2	3	4	5
Student used varied resources.	1	2	3	4	5
Student's research was extensive.	1	2	3	4	5
Student developed a fine product.	1	2	3	4	5
Student's class presentation was effective.	1	2	3	4	5
I have good feelings about the student's independent study.	1	2	3	4	5

What was done well: _____

_____

_____

_____

Areas that need improving: _____

_____

_____

_____

EVALUATE ME!

(Evaluation by Audience)

Presenter(s) _____ Date _____

Topic _____

Directions: Check (√) the line that best describes how you feel about each phrase.

The presenter:

	YES	NOT SURE	NO
spoke clearly	—	—	—
looked at the audience	—	—	—
told the study question	—	—	—
answered the study question	—	—	—
made the information understandable	—	—	—
used a visual aid	—	—	—

I learned _____

_____

The most interesting part of the presentation was _____

_____

Why? _____

_____

In the lesson I:

__ listened   __ asked questions
__ discussed   __ answered question
__ read something   __ made something
__ other _____

Questions I have about the study: _____

_____

_____